How to Be A Gentleman

In 7 Days

A Crash Course in Etiquette

Crombie Jardine
PUBLISHING LIMITED

13 Nonsuch Walk, Cheam, Surrey, SM2 7LG
www.crombiejardine.com

Published by Crombie Jardine Publishing Limited
First edition, 2005

ISBN 1-905102-16-X

Designed by 'Mr Stiffy'
Printed & bound in the United Kingdom by
William Clowes Ltd, Beccles, Suffolk

CONTENTS

DAY 2: SOCIAL BEHAVIOUR, ANTI-SOCIAL BEHAVIOUR, WINING AND DINING 35

DAY 5: EDUCATION FOR GENTLEMEN ... 100

DAY 6: MARRYING WELL, PROPOSING, CRYING OFF, KEEPING THE RING ETC..... 123

DEFINING THE GENTLEMAN

Gentleman (from Old English gentilman, meaning nobleman; gentil = noble.)

- A gentleman is well born i.e. of good family (in other words, he's a cut above your average yeoman.

- A gentleman is well bred and has gentle manners.

- A British gentleman bears arms, but has no title.

- An American gentleman is well read, well educated and well off.

- A real or proper gent is both a gent by birth and a gent by nature.

- It should be noted that not all gentlemen actually behave like gentlemen. Many act in a supercilious or superior fashion and look down on commoners. They are rude to trades people, employees and the like, mistake snobbish and pretentious behaviour for good breeding, are generally without good manners and are invariably two-faced. In fact, these gentlemen are not gentlemen at all.

• In modern times anyone can be a gentleman. Yet many ordinary men seem at loss how to behave like one.

What is the definition of a gentleman?
One who knows how to play the banjo but chooses not to.

INTRODUCTION

Have you noticed that there's a lot of anti-men feeling around at the moment?

Just take this for an example:

A woman once said that a man is like a deck of cards.

You need:

- **a Heart to love him**
- **a Diamond to marry him**
- **a Club to smash his stupid head in**
- **a Spade to bury the bastard.**

Just what have men been up to that they're being dealt such a bad hand? They are really not in the good books at all these days. In fact, they are even getting a bad press in the Good Book itself:

One day in the Garden of Eden, Eve called out to God. 'Lord, I know that you created me and provided this beautiful garden and all these wonderful animals, but I'm just not happy. And I'm sick to death of apples.'

'Well then, Eve,' said God, 'I shall create a man for you.'

'What's a man?' asked Eve.

'A creature that is bigger, stronger and faster than you and will satisfy your needs. But since you complained about your lot, there is a catch. He will only satisfy your physical needs on occasion and your mental needs on very rare occasion. In fact, you'll often be more frustrated than when you had only the animals for company. He will also get you with child, and you will give birth, and it will hurt like hell. On top of this, man will lie, cheat and be vain. He will like to hunt and kill things. He will look silly when he is aroused. He will be witless and will revel in childish things like fighting and kicking a ball about.'

'Eh, sounds great,' said Eve, hesitantly. 'Are there any more catches?'

'Yes,' said God. 'Man will be proud, arrogant and vain . . . so you'll have to let him believe that I made him first, and that you were his idea. You'll have to get used to him getting it wrong by the way. We'll keep it our secret. You know, woman to woman.'

Men, you have got to shape up a bit, and put an end to these attacks on manhood. And you've got seven days in which to do it. Remember God created a whole world in that time.

Why does a penis have a hole in the end? **So men can be open minded.**

DAY 1

GETTING OUT OF BED, BREAKFAST, PERSONAL HYGIENE AND BATHROOM ETIQUETTE

Did you know…?

Most men have erections every 60 to 90 minutes during sleep.

WAKING UP

Your alarm clock goes off at 7 o'clock...

YOU DO NOT:

- Switch it off, lie back on the pillow and begin snoring.
- Stretch your arms the entire width of the bed while yawning loudly and hit the person beside you in the eye.
- Ask the person beside you to wake you up in ten minutes with a cup of tea.
- Ask the person beside you if they fancy a quick one.
- Scratch your bollocks and/or backside.
- Admire your morn horn.
- Fart.

YOU DO:

- Exit quietly from the room without disturbing your partner if they do not need to get up yet.
- Gently wake your partner if they do.
- Offer to make your partner a cup of tea.

GETTING OUT OF BED

Swing your legs neatly around so that you are in a sitting position, place hands either side of you and push up from the bed. There is no need to test the springs by using your entire weight to bounce you out of the bed. Or to bounce your partner out of the bed. Beds should be aired well before being made – by you that is. However, there is no need to pull the covers away from your partner if they are still asleep.

GOING TO THE BATHROOM

When you rise and shine in the morning, do not make a point of boasting about your morning glory to the woman lying beside you. She won't be interested when you have morning breath to match. Do not ever be tempted to try it on if she is asleep. This is extremely ungentlemanly behaviour. Just forget last night's dreams and remind yourself that you need a pee. Hurry off to the bathroom and relieve yourself – quietly!

HOW TO PEE POLITELY

1. Lift the lid and the loo seat – quietly.
   There's no need to bang the lid on
   the tank and drop the seat three
   times. Come on lads, you've been
   at this since you were wee boys.

2. No matter how heavy-lidded you may be,
   keep your eye on the job. Aim straight.
   No gentleman pees on the bathroom
   tiles. (No gentleman has such a thing as
   a bathroom carpet by the way!) Should
   there be an overspill, on no account
   clean it up with the bathroom towel!

3. Pee quietly. In other words, no moaning,
   groaning or grunting. That first pee
   of the day sounds like the Niagara
   Falls all by itself, thank you.

4. Try to rein in any gas. I know you're
   in the loo chaps, but if your partner is
   within earshot, it will put her off you
   before your day has even begun.

5. **ABSOLUTELY NO WANKING BEFORE BREAKFAST!**

6. **FLUSH THE CHAIN!**

7. Return the loo seat and lid to the original position. Ladies HATE falling down the toilet bowl, especially one you've just peed in.

GOING DOWNSTAIRS

If you sleep naked then put on your pyjamas
or dressing gown now. The neighbours should
not have to suffer your nudity when you take in
the milk. Otherwise, put your dressing gown
over your pyjamas. This should be of good
quality. It should not show any signs of:

- **England football team logos or the like.**

- **The name of the hotel from
  which it was stolen.**

- **Yesterday's breakfast stains.**

- **Any other stains.**

If you must wear slippers, please no
Garfield fluffies, granddad-type, or ones
with beer mugs or footballs on them.

'There is a vast difference between the savage and the civilised man, but it is never apparent to their wives until after breakfast.'
Helen Rowland

'A bachelor's life is a fine breakfast, a flat lunch, and a miserable dinner.'
Francis Bacon

'Oysters are the usual opening to a winter breakfast. Indeed, they are almost indispensable.'
Grimod de la Reynière

BREAKFAST

MENU

Kippers
Kidneys
Eggs
Bacon
Crisp toast
Gentlemen's marmalade
Orange or tomato juice
Fresh coffee
Fine-blend tea

You may read your broadsheet newspaper at the breakfast table if you so wish. Remember that not everyone likes to chat in the morning – particularly about the size of a page-three girl's breasts. Refrain from putting on the television or playing loud music.

Sit up at the table or breakfast bar. Do not slouch on the couch. Use both your knife and fork. Do not talk with your mouth full, shovel food into your mouth (even if late for work), belch or fart at the table.

SHOWERING

A brisk, cold shower should invigorate sleepy
brain cells. Do remember that there is no need to
flood the entire bathroom, or to spray the mirrors,
ceiling and windows while rinsing your face after
shaving. Do wipe up any mess – not with bathroom
towels! Do not leave bathroom towels on the floor.

*'See the problem is that God has given
men a brain and a penis, and only
enough blood to run one at a time.'*
Robin Williams

DO:

- Hang up / put away pyjamas and dressing gown. If PJs need washing place in laundry basket.

- Make sure curtain is pulled across – so that the water doesn't go on the floor, not so that you can get away with any insalubrious shower habits.

- Wet shave without cutting yourself.

- Wash well – including under arms, privates and feet.

- Wash – and condition – hair.

- Leave enough hot water for anyone else to wash with.

- Turn off the shower.

- Use a bathmat, not a clean towel to stand on.

- Check the soap is hair free.

- Wipe up excess water – not with bathroom towels.

- Dry yourself on expensive white towels and place them in the laundry basket. If you are ecologically friendly, return them to the towel rack instead.

- Brush hair with clean hairbrush.

- Restrain the amount of hair gel used.

- Use anti-perspirant or deodorant.

- Clean teeth.

- Check ears for hair and wax.

- Brush hair.

- Trim nails if necessary.

- Open the bathroom window if the room has steamed up.

- Use an air freshener if you have polluted the bathroom atmosphere.

- Check the loo to make sure all incriminating evidence has flushed away. (N.B. Gentlemen never leave skid marks!)

- Shut the bathroom window before leaving for work.

DO NOT:

- Use your partner's face cloth, loofah, facemask, dilapidating cream, conditioner, leg-shaving gel, lady-shave razors or the like.

- Sing out of tune.

- Fart.

THE BATHROOM ROUTINE OF AN UNGENTLEMANLY MALE . . .

Take off dressing gown and pyjamas and
leave them in a pile on the bedroom floor.

Walk naked to the bathroom.

Should you see partner on the way, shake penis
at her while making 'woo-woo' sounds.

Pick nose and flick the pickings.

Get in the shower. Turn tap on full blast
before pulling curtain across.

Blow nose in hands and let water rinse them off.

Fart and laugh at how loud it sounds in the shower.

Sing loudly and very flatly using the wrong words.

Wash face, but spend majority of
time washing privates.

Make a Shampoo Mohawk.

Rinse badly.

Get out of shower.

Partially dry off.

Leave towel on floor and partially
covering water on floor.

Rub off steamed up mirror to check
face, admire size of penis gain etc.

Leave shower curtain open and bathroom light on.

No need to think about shutting window,
as you never thought to open window.

Return to bedroom with towel around waist. If
you pass partner, pull off towel, shake penis at
her and make the 'woo-woo' sound again.

Throw wet towel on bed.

HOW TO WET SHAVE

Wet the face with hot water. When hair absorbs hot water it becomes softer and easier to cut, while hot water relaxes facial muscles.

Dip a good quality badger shaving brush into hot water.

Place some shaving foam in one's hand and, using a circular motion, build up a rich creamy lather on the brush.

Apply the lather to the beard, allowing the brush to lift the beard and make the hairs stand proud.

The brush may be dipped lightly into hot water if more moisture is required in the lather.

If using shaving soap, dip the brush in hot water and use a similar circular motion on the soap to create a rich lather.

Use a good blade that has been warmed under hot running water. Shave the face in the direction of the beard growth (this is important to avoid shaving rash, ingrown hairs, razor burn, nicks, cuts, bleeding and bits of toilet paper stuck to your face for most of the morning).

Rinse the blade in hot water frequently as you shave.

Rinse the face thoroughly with cool
water and pat dry with a soft towel.

Did you know…?

*Beards are the fastest growing hairs
on the human body.*

*If the average man never trimmed his
beard, it would grow to nearly 30 feet
long in his lifetime.*

MAKING THE BED

Plump up the pillows. Take one corner of the duvet
– there are four of them – and pull to the top corner
of the bed. Match up each corner of the duvet in
this way to each corner of the bed. Smooth any
wrinkles by running your hand across the top.

GETTING DRESSED

If working in an office, put on a clean, ironed shirt,
with the full complement of buttons. Wear a non-
clashing tie – no fish, beer-cans etc. Wear sensible
socks – no Manchester United logos, cartoon
characters etc. Shoes should have been polished
the night before to avoid polish on clean clothes
and under clean nails. Check shoulders of suit for
dandruff, brush off if necessary. Remove stray hairs
and fluff from suit. Avoid hairy animals on your way
out of the door. Wish your partner a good day, but
be careful of her lipstick. On no account be tempted
to try a quickie. You just showered and dressed for
goodness sake! Besides which you'll be late for work.

THINGS TO REMEMBER BEFORE LEAVING THE HOUSE

- Briefcase

- Clean handkerchief

- Train times

- Way to the office

- Not to fart on the Underground

- Give old ladies and pregnant women your seat on the bus or train

- Book the theatre and dinner afterwards

- Buy your mother a birthday card

- Don't be home later than you said without calling your partner

- Buy your partner some chocolates or flowers (not supermarket-own brand, garage floristry or cheap carnations).

The only seat available on the train was next to a well-dressed, middle-aged French woman and the seat was occupied by her dog. The weary American traveller asked, 'Ma'am, please would you move your dog. I need that seat.' The French woman looked down her nose at the American, sniffed and said, 'You Americans. You are such a rude class of people. Can't you see my little FiFi is using that seat?'

The American walked away, determined to find a place to rest, but after another trip up and down the train carriage he found himself again facing the woman with the dog. Again he asked, 'Please, lady. May I sit there? I'm very tired.'

The French woman wrinkled her nose and snorted. 'You Americans! Not only are you rude, you are also arrogant... Imagine!'

The American didn't say anything else. He leaned over, picked up the dog, tossed it out the window of the train and sat down in the empty seat. The woman shrieked, and begged someone to defend her honour and chastise the American.

An Englishman sitting across the aisle spoke up indignantly, 'You know, sir, you Americans do seem to have a penchant for doing the wrong thing. You eat holding the fork in the wrong hand. You drive your cars on the wrong side of the road. And now you've thrown the wrong bitch out the window.'

DAY 2

SOCIAL BEHAVIOUR, ANTI-SOCIAL BEHAVIOUR, WINING AND DINING

'A true gentleman is one who is never unintentionally rude.'
Oscar Wilde

A true gentleman is the sort that is sincere in word and deed, honest as the day is long, courageous, altruistic etc. However, some gentlemen are so polished in the art of gentlemanship that they are just one big act. If you want to be a gentleman aspire to the former. If, however, you wish to rise up a notch on the social scale take note of the following...

GENTLEMEN ALWAYS . . .

- Buy their new clothes in Savile Row.
- Belong to a club.
- Discuss their days at Eton and Harrow with fellow Etonians and Harovians.
- Go fishing and sailing in the summer and

shooting in colder seasons. (Apparently, gentlemen do not ski – Prince Charles and sons rank higher than gentlemen, of course.)

- Hold doors open for people unnecessarily.

- Say 'Good Morning' to other gentlefolk, although maybe not to the lower classes.

- Say 'Good Morning' to people they do not like.

- Can be supercilious in their greeting habits and can greet each other like long-lost lovers upon first introduction.

- Stand up and offer their seat to a lady.

- Offer to carry what a lady is carrying, even if she seems to be coping well with her load.

- Offer ladies their arm.

- Walk on the traffic side of the road.

- Place folded handkerchiefs in their breast pockets, but are never seen to blow their noses on them.

- Ask if anyone objects before lighting a cigarette.

- Stand up if a lady leaves the room.

GENTLEMEN NEVER...

- Hit ladies.
- Discuss money.
- Carry money – otherwise what are accounts and dining cards for?
- Follow fashion other than their own.
- Start pub fights.
- Brawl in the street.
- Eat in the street.
- Let themselves be observed in altercations with their next-door neighbours.
- Shout at other drivers – they have a chauffeur for that sort of thing.
- Cheat at cards or dice games.
- Confuse the use of the 'V' sign.
- Relieve themselves in the street (unless after the rugby).

WHAT'S IN A NAME?

Gentlemen are called	Gentlemen are rarely called
Percival	Romeo
Harry	Wayne
John	Chuck
Piers (though there was a Piers the ploughman)	Dave
Algernon	Tyler
George	Gary
Giles	Kevin
Gregory	Bradley
Anthony	Tyson
Francis	Neil
Henry	Trevor
William	Scott
Hubert	Shane

Those wishing to check up on family names, should consult *Burke's Peerage & Gentry* – a guide to the titled families of Great Britain and Ireland.

MEETING AND GREETING

HOW TO CONDUCT YOURSELF

Gentleman should to some extent follow the example of 'When in Rome do as the Romans do'. On the other hand, while on the continent a bit of hugging and air-kissing is acceptable, many British gentlemen usually show a greater degree of reserve (self-restraint being evidence of good character). Such gentlemen will be happy to shake your hand or nod a greeting to you, but they will not appreciate being slapped on the back or greeted with the words, 'All right, mate?' or 'How's it hanging?' You have to learn to spot the stiff-upper-lip sort of gent and treat him as he thinks he deserves.

Similarly, while displays of backslapping are to be observed in public schools and on building sites equally, never indulge in such gestures in polite company. Besides which, a respectable distance should be observed during formal conversation

– especially with ladies, many of whom do not appreciate their arms and shoulders being touched by strangers. Play it safe and let them initiate any physical contact. The days of kissing her hand are well and truly over by the way; you'll seem pretentious or silly if you start that.

When talking to another gentleman or indeed to a lady, look at them. Even if they are the utmost bore, or very ugly, it is not polite to let your eyes wander, particularly in the direction of the pretty blonde in the too-short dress. Even if you're bored rigid, pretend you are interested in what the other person is saying. When you have got through a few minutes of conversation, make a polite excuse, say goodbye and move on.

'Questioning is not the mode of conversation among gentlemen.'
Samuel Johnson

MEETING AND GREETING FAUX PAS

DO NOT...

- Talk too loudly.
- Crack jokes.
- Laugh uproariously.
- Talk with your mouth full.
- Butt in on someone else's anecdote.
- Hog the conversation.
- Make personal comments.
- Answer your mobile phone while someone is talking to you.
- Shuffle your feet constantly.
- Gesture wildly, especially while holding a drink; on the other hand do not stand with your hands in your pockets (historically, when gentleman carried arms, this made people understandably nervous).
- Behave like a bore or boor.
- Talk exclusively about yourself. 'How do you do?' is a greeting not a question.

DINNER IS SERVED

Table manners play an important part in
making a favourable impression. Good
table manners denote good breeding.

NAPKINS . . .

Never start your meal until your host unfolds
his or her napkin. When you see them do
so, unfold your own and place it on your lap
– completely open if you are attending a small
luncheon party, or in half and lengthwise if you
are eating dinner and have been supplied with a
dinner napkin the size of a small tablecloth.

Keep your napkin on your lap throughout the
entire meal, unless you wish to dab at the corners
of your mouth occasionally. Never blow your
nose on your napkin, or fan yourself with it, even
if you are sweltering in your dinner jacket.

If you need to leave the table during the meal, place your napkin on your chair. Placing it on the table means that you have finished your meal, and you may come back and find yourself without dessert.

The meal is over, by the way, not when you have had enough to eat, or have got bored of the conversation, but when the host places his or her napkin on the table. You too should place your napkin neatly on the table - to the right of your dinner plate. Do not refold your napkin, however. No one else wants it after it has been near your lips and warming your groin.

THE MENU . . .

Sometimes it is best to order what you know and
what you know how to eat. For example, if you have
never eaten a lobster or snails, don't do so for the first
time when you are trying to make a good impression.
However, if the menu is in French without a
translation, and you don't speak it, you may have
to pick something and grin and bear it. Otherwise
you could always ask the waiter to recommend a
dish, or ask the other dinner guests if anyone has
eaten at the restaurant before and if so whether
they would recommend anything in particular.

N.B. When ordering you should wait your
turn. The waiter will ask you, probably
after he has asked any ladies present.

N.B. Gentlemen do not ask if the fish comes
in batter, or the chips with curry sauce.

BREAD ROLLS...

Remembering the rule 'liquids on your right, solids
on your left' will save you the embarrassment
of eating someone else's bread roll or drinking
from someone else's glass. The bread roll
should be broken with one's fingers by the
way, not sawn in half with the butter knife.

*'. . . it is a great breach of etiquette
when your fingers are dirty and
greasy, to bring them to your mouth in
order to lick them, or to clean them on
your jacket.
It would be more decent to
use the tablecloth.'*
**Erasmus,
Treatise on Manners, 1530**

'Put not your meat to your
Mouth with your Knife in
your hand neither Spit forth
the Stones of any fruit Pye
upon a Dish nor Cast
anything under
the table.'
George Washington

THE SILVERWARE...

If you remember the rule 'outside in' you can't go wrong.

Start with the knife, fork, or spoon that is farthest from your plate, then work your way in, using one utensil for each course. The spoon above your plate is for your dessert, not for your soup. Use both your knife and fork, eating each mouthful as it is cut. It is not acceptable to chop up all your food first and then to shovel it in with a fork only. Neither is it acceptable to lick one's knife. Never put a piece of used silverware back on the tablecloth. After you have finished with the food on your plate, arrange your knife and fork together and lay them diagonally across the plate. Vertically is probably OK too, but not pointing in different directions and spread across the plate. Do not shove the plate away.

By the way, the first utensil was the dagger, which is why we don't point knives at people sitting with us at the table, and why, in 1669, King Louis XIV of France ordered that all table knives should have rounded ends.

FORMAL DINNER PLACE SETTING

1. Napkin

2. Fish Fork

3. Main Course Fork

4. Salad Fork

5. Soup Bowl and Plate

6. Dinner Plate

7. Dinner Knife

8. Fish Knife

9. Soup Spoon

10. Bread and Butter Plate

11. Butter Knife

12. Desert silverware

13. Water Glass

14. Red Wine Glass

15. White Wine Glass

HOW TO EAT SOUP

- Check you have the soup spoon
  and not the dessert spoon.

- If the soup is too hot to swallow, wait till it
  cools down a bit. If you burn your mouth
  you won't be able to taste your next course,
  besides which it is bad form to either spit out a
  boiling mouthful or to blow on one's soup.

- Never break up your bread and float it in your soup.

- Never lift your soup plate to your
  mouth and drink out of it.

- Never slurp soup.

- Push your soup spoon to the far edge of
  the bowl when spooning soup; otherwise
  it might splatter your tie. Similarly, if you
  must tilt your bowl, tilt it away from you.

- Never serve too much soup to guests – they
  may get the idea that you cannot afford meat.

- Traditionally, gentlemen never
  take soup at luncheon.

∼ NOT STUCK FOR WORDS ∼

The wonderfully absent-minded Lord Dudley used to rehearse conversations to himself out loud, using two voices, one gruff and one shrill.

One day, Dudley was asked to present a country gentleman at court. As they were leaving the palace, their carriage was stuck in a traffic jam.

Suddenly the country gentleman was startled to hear Dudley saying, 'Now this tiresome country squire will be expecting me to ask him to dine. Shall I? Or shall I not? On the whole I think not. I think he might be a bore.'

Not to be dismissed in this peculair way, the astonished squire rejoined, 'Now this tiresome old peer will of course be asking me to dine with him today. Shall I or not? No. I am pretty sure it would be a bore.'

Dudley, shocked, but seeing the humour in the situation, asked the squire to dine with him.

TO RECAP, GENTLEMEN . . .

- Say grace (briefly and in Latin).

- Have a cook and a butler.

- Know how to eat soup, fish and
  fowl in the correct manner.

- Know their vintages – i.e. can order a good
  and complementary bottle of wine (not
  to be confused with complimentary).

- Are familiar with the flatware
  and silverware.

- Always have linen napkins, china plates,
  silver cutlery and crystal glasses.

- Dab their mouths with a napkin.

- Never blow their noses on the napkin.

- Never drink red and white wine
  from the same glass.

- Can translate a French menu.

- Do not pick their teeth at the table.

- Do not rest their elbows on the table.

- Do not overstuff themselves (this leads to belching, farting and having to answer a call of nature during the after-dinner speeches).

- Do not throw food (except during bun fights at Oxford and Cambridge).

- Discuss the opera and ballet, but never discuss politics, religion or sex at the dinner table.

- Pass the port to the left.

- Never belch at the dinner table.

- Never fart at the dinner table.

- Always say 'Excuse me' when leaving the dinner table for a pee but never say 'Just going for a pee.'

- Always thank the hostess and admire the food and wine – even if both are terrible.

- Always send round a hand-written thank-you note the following day.

A gentleman enters his favourite restaurant and sits at his regular table.

Looking around, he notices a gorgeous lady sitting at a table nearby, all alone. He calls the waiter over and asks him to send their most expensive bottle of Merlot over to her. The waiter gets the bottle and takes it over to the woman, saying, 'This is from the gentleman over there,' indicating to him.

She regards the wine coolly for a second and decides to send a note over to the man. The waiter conveys it to the gentleman. The note reads: 'For me to accept this bottle, you need to have a Mercedes in your garage, a million dollars in the bank, and 7 inches in your pants.'

After reading the note, the man composes one of his own. He hands it to the waiter and instructs him to return this to the lady. It reads: 'For your information - I happen to have a Ferrari Testarossa, an Aston Martin DB7 and a Mercedes SL55 in my garage; plus I have over twenty million in the bank. But not even for a woman as beautiful as you would I cut off three inches.'

EUPHEMISMS FOR GOING TO THE GENTS, IF YOU REALLY MUST BE EXCUSED FROM THE TABLE:

- I must go and answer the call of nature.
- I must go and pick a rose.
- I just need to send a telegram.
- I'm off to chase a rabbit.
- I'm off to shoot a lion.
- I need to see a man about a horse.
- Just off to spike the punch.
- Just off to visit that good man St. John.

Did you know…?

*The average person releases
nearly a pint of intestinal gas
by flatulence every day. Most
of this is due to swallowed air.
The rest is from fermentation
of undigested food.*

Ps & Qs

GENTLEMEN NEVER SUFFER FROM
FOOT-IN-MOUTH DISEASE. WATCH
YOUR WORDS WITH CARE.

As a shy gentleman was preparing to board
a plane, he heard that the Pope was on the
same flight. 'This is exciting,' thought the
gentleman, 'I've always been a big fan of the
Pope. Perhaps I'll be able to see him in person.'

Imagine his surprise when the Pope sat down
in the seat next to him for the flight. Still, the
gentleman was too shy to speak to the Pontiff.

Shortly after takeoff, the Pope began
a crossword puzzle. 'This is fantastic,'
thought the gentleman, 'I'm really
good at crosswords. Perhaps if the Pope
gets stuck, he'll ask me for help.'

Almost immediately, the Pope turned to
the gentleman and said, 'Excuse me, but
do you know a four letter word referring
to a woman that ends in u-n-t?'

Only one word leapt to mind. 'My goodness,' thought the gentleman, 'I can't tell the Pope that. There must be another.' The gentleman thought for quite a while, then it hit him. Turning to the Pope, the gentleman said, 'I think you're looking for the word "aunt".' 'Of course,' said the Pope. 'Do you have an eraser?'

A man walked into the produce section of his local supermarket and asked to buy half a head of lettuce. The boy working in that department told him that they only sold whole heads of lettuce.

The man was insistent that the boy ask his manager about the matter. Walking into the back room, the boy said to his manager, 'Some asshole wants to buy a half a head of lettuce.' As he finished his sentence, he turned to find the man standing right behind him, so he added, 'and this gentleman kindly offered to

buy the other half.' The manager approved
the deal and the man went on his way.

Later the manager found the boy and said, 'I was
impressed with the way you got yourself out of
that situation earlier. We like people who think
on their feet here. Where are you from son?'

'Canada, Sir,' the boy replied.

'Well, why did you leave Canada?'
the manager asked.

The boy said, 'Sir, there's nothing but
whores and hockey players up there.'

'Really!' said the manager. 'My wife is Canadian.'

The boy replied, 'No kidding?
Who did she play for?'

DAY 3

THE CUT OF YOUR CLOTH,
WHAT TO WEAR TO GRAND OCCASIONS,
BALLS AND BALLS-UPS...

A gentleman should observe the correct dress on every occasion – usually not ripped jeans and a Man United or Arsenal T-shirt.

How to Tie a Bow Tie

Adjust the tie so that one end is slightly longer than the other, and cross the long end over the short.

Bring the long end through the middle at the neck.

Form a loop with the short end of the
tie crossing left. Drop the long end at
the neck over this horizontal loop.

Form a similarly angled loop with the loose long end
of the tie and push this loop through the short loop.

Tighten the knot by adjusting the ends of both loops.

You may find that it takes several
attempts at first, but stick with it.

WHAT TO WEAR TO GRAND OCCASIONS

* Morning dress

Morning dress comprises morning tailcoat, trousers and waistcoat. Shoes should be black, and socks either black or grey, depending on the colour of your trousers. The safest colour of shirt is white. Your choice of tie depends on the occasion: a funeral or memorial service requires black; a wedding offers the chance for something a little brighter – but not vulgar!

* A black tie do

A black tuxedo coat, black formal trousers (with satin outseam), a white formal shirt, a vest or cummerbund with coordinating tie, button studs and cuff links, black dress shoes.

* A white tie do

Evening tailcoat, trousers, white shirt, white waistcoat, white bow-tie, white button studs and cuff links, black formal shoes, white gloves (optional).

* 'Dinner Jacket' invitations

White dinner jacket, black formal trousers, white formal shirt, vest or cummerbund with coordinating tie, black dress shoes.

* Royal Ascot

Morning dress and a top hat. Treat your wife or girlfriend to a nice hat as well, and traditionally a dress below the knee.

* Glyndebourne (opera)

A dinner jacket and black tie (preferably not a white tuxedo).

* A debutante ball

White tie, black tie or dinner jacket – as specified on the invitation.

* Dinner at your club

Many gentlemen's clubs and smarter hotels and restaurants still require gentlemen to wear a jacket and tie.

GENTLEMEN DO NOT...

- Carry pens in their jacket breast pockets. (An ornamental silk handkerchief is more like it.)

- Wear ties belonging to institutions to which they themselves do not belong.

- Wear polyester ties.

- Wear bow ties on elastic.

- Pay their tailors.

WHAT TO DO IF YOU'VE GOT IT WRONG

- Pretend you have come from another party.

- Borrow a jacket and tie from the restaurant.

- Claim to be at the wrong event and hurry away home.

WHAT TO DO IF YOU FART WHEN ATTEMPTING A BOW

- Blame it on your squeaky shoes.

- Turn to the person next to you and say that you heard it but they shouldn't be embarrassed.

- Blame the floorboards in these old houses.

- Feign a coughing fit and hope it makes people think that they heard the wrong end.

- Kick the dog.

WHAT TO DO IF YOU FART IN A LIFT

- Enjoy it.

At Heathrow, a 300-foot-long red carpet is stretched out to Air Force One and President Bush strides to a warm, but dignified handshake from Queen Elizabeth II.

They ride in a silver 1934 Bentley limousine to the edge of central London where they board an open 17th-century coach hitched to six magnificent white matching horses. They ride toward Buckingham Palace, each looking sideways and waving to the thousands of cheering Brits lining the streets. All is going well.

Suddenly the right rear horse lets fly with the most horrendous, earth-rending, eye-smarting blast of gastronomic flatulence ever heard in the British Empire, including Bermuda, Tortola and the Falkland Islands. It shakes the coach. Uncomfortable, but in control, the two dignitaries of state do their best to ignore the whole incident.

The Queen then turns to Mr Bush and says, 'Mr President, please accept my regrets. I'm sure you understand that there are some things that even a Queen cannot control.' George W. Bush, ever the gentleman, replies, 'Your Majesty, please don't give the matter another thought. You know, if you hadn't said something, I would have thought it was one of the horses...'

HOW TO ADDRESS ROYALTY

Rank	Term of Address
King	Your Majesty
Queen	Your Majesty
Prince and Princess	Your Royal Highness
Duke and Duchess	Your Grace
Marquess	My Lord
Marchioness	Madam
Earl	My Lord
Countess	Madam
Viscount	My Lord
Viscountess	Madam
Baron	My Lord
Baroness	Madam

*'Everyone likes flattery,
and when it comes to royalty,
you should lay it on
with a trowel.'*
Benjamin Disraeli

HOW TO TELL IF YOU'VE DRUNK TOO MUCH

- You drop your posh accent.

- You laugh too loudly and too long.

- You become lewd and lascivious.

- You shout at the waiter, as if he were deaf.

- You lose your grandfather's lighter
  and resort to buying a cheap
  throwaway in shocking pink.

- You ask the waitress to dinner.

- You forget you are engaged to be married.

- You eat a kebab.

- You begin to sing football anthems.

DAY 4

REGARD FOR THE OTHER SEX, HOW TO SPOT A LADY, DATING AND ROMANCING

'A man who will not lie to a woman has very little consideration for her feelings.'
Olin Miller

*'Women need a reason to have sex.
Men just need a place.'*
Billy Crystal

*'I really think that American
gentlemen are the best after all,
because kissing your hand may make
you feel very good but a diamond and
a sapphire bracelet lasts forever.'*
Anita Loos

A REMINDER OF WHAT THE OTHER SEX THINKS OF THE AVERAGE MAN

Men are like laxatives...

they irritate the shit out of you.

Men are like bananas...

the older they get, the less firm they are.

Men are like holidays...

they never seem to be long enough.

Men are like the weather...

nothing can be done to change them.

Men are like blenders...

you need one, but you're not quite sure why.

Men are like chocolate…

sweet, smooth, and they usually head
right for your hips.

Men are like commercials…

you can't believe a word they say.

Men are like department stores…

their clothes are always 1/2 off.

Men are like government bonds…

they take so long to mature.

Men are like mascara…

they usually run at the first sign of emotion.

Men are like popcorn...

they satisfy you, but only for a little while.

Men are like snowstorms...

you never know when they're coming, how many inches you'll get or how long it will last.

Men are like lava lamps...

fun to look at, but not very bright.

Men are like parking spots...

all the good ones are taken.

NO GENTLEMAN WOULD EVER LAUGH OUT LOUD AT THE FOLLOWING:

How many men does it take to open a beer?

*None. It should have been opened
by the time she brings it.*

Why do women have smaller feet than men?

So they can stand closer to the kitchen sink.

How do you know when a woman is
about to say something smart?

*When she starts her sentence with
'A man once told me…'*

How do you fix a woman's watch?

You don't. There is a clock on the oven.

What doesn't belong in this list:
meat, eggs, wife, blowjob?

*Blowjob: You can beat your meat, eggs or
wife, but you can't beat a blowjob.*

Why do men break wind more than women?

*Because women can't shut up long enough
to build up the required pressure.*

If your dog is barking at the back door and your wife
is yelling at the front door, whom do you let in first?

The dog, of course. He'll shut up once you let him in.

What's worse than a male chauvinist pig?

A woman who won't do what she's told.

What does 'wife' stand for?

Washing, Ironing, Fucking, Etc.

On a transatlantic flight, a plane passes
through a severe storm. The turbulence is
awful, and things go from bad to worse
when one wing is struck by lightning.

One woman in particular loses it and
starts screaming, 'I'm too young to die.'
Then she yells, 'Well, if I'm going to die, I
want my last minutes to be memorable!
Is there anyone on this plane who
can make me feel like a woman?'

For a moment there is silence. Everyone
stares at the desperate woman in the front
of the plane. Then an Italian man stands
up in the rear of the plane. He is gorgeous:
tall, well built, with dark brown hair and
eyes. He starts to walk slowly up the aisle,
unbuttoning his shirt, one button at a time.
No one moves. He removes his shirt. Muscles
ripple across his chest. The woman gasps.

He whispers: 'Iron this, and get
me something to eat.'

HOW TO SPOT A LADY

A lady does not have…

- A beard
- Coat-hanger shoulders
- Narrow hips
- An Adam's Apple
- A deep voice
- Fake breasts
- Huge feet
- A bulge in her trousers
- Hairy hands
- Have a false tan

A lady does not...

- Wear too much make-up
- Bleach her hair
- Pass wind in public
- Pick her nose
- Get plastered
- Belch
- Sit with her legs open or crossed
- Wear over-tight or revealing clothes
- Gossip
- Talk with her mouth full
- Order the most expensive thing in the restaurant
- Wear fake jewellery

A GENTLEMAN'S DATING ETIQUETTE

- On public outings, only take out ladies, although you may take whomsoever you wish to private parties.

- It is the done thing to pick up the lady from her home and escort her, preferably in a nice car, to the chosen venue.

- If she is still living with her parents, do your best to charm them – it will go down well. Smile warmly, shake hands with them, address them as 'Mr' and 'Mrs', thank them for sparing their daughter for an evening, for example.

- If driving, open the car door for her both when she gets in and out of the car.

- Compliment her on her appearance, but don't get too specific.

- Hold open the door of the restaurant, club, theatre, wherever.

- If the chap at the cloakroom doesn't do so, help her off with her coat.

- Check she is seated comfortably/has a

programme/has a drink/is cool or warm
enough/likes the menu etc. etc.

- Introduce your date to your friends. Make
  it clear to her that you are happy to do so,
  but on no account engage in nudge, nudge,
  wink, wink asides to your friends.

- Do not allow your friends to be rude to your date.

- Never discuss her physical charms
  with them in front of her.

- On no account abandon your date to talk to your
  friends, especially for long periods at a party.

- At a dinner party, ensure that she is included in the
  conversation. She is not there just so you could say
  you brought someone, or to be ogled by your mates.

- Make sure that you listen to her during dinner;
  neither shout her down, deluge her with your
  opinions on life, the universe, your ideal woman
  and everything; and never, ever insult her mother.

- Should she be cooking for you, eat
  everything and say you liked it, even if you
  were desperate to give it to her cat.

- Cats. Women like them so be nice
  about cats – and never kick them.

- Check she has had enough to eat, what
  time she would like to go home etc.

- On no account get her drunk.

- On no account sleep with her on the first
  date. Gentlemen show restraint.

- Offer to walk her/drive her/accompany
  her in a taxi to her home. However, there
  is no need on a first date to stay for coffee,
  unless you are sure you just mean coffee.

- Call her the next day, like you said you would.

- If you really want to impress, send
  flowers and thank her for the date.

- Never invite your wife and
  mistress to the same party.

UNGENTLEMANLY CHAT-UP LINES

• The bulge in my trousers has your name on it.

• Nice legs. . . what time do they open?

• You've got 206 bones in your body, want one more?

• You might not be the best-looking girl here,
  but beauty is only a light switch away.

• Can I buy you a drink or do you
  just want the money?

• Want to meet me round the back?

• Do you have a mirror in your knickers
  because I can see myself in them?

• There's a cheap motel I know. . .

• I really like that outfit. It would look
  great on my bedroom floor.

• What would you like for breakfast?

*'I don't like compliments, and I don't
see why a man should think he is
pleasing a woman enormously when
he says to her a whole heap of things
that he doesn't mean.'*
Oscar Wilde

GENTLEMANLY WAYS TO LET A
GIRL DOWN NICELY

- You deserve a real gentleman, not a cad like me.

- You deserve someone who'd treat you like a lady.

- I'd love to share my worldly goods
  with you, only there aren't any.

- I wouldn't want you to have to suffer my family.

- The family jewels aren't in good working order.

- I love you, but I love my horse more.

- We've had a few problems with inbreeding, you
  know. Nothing much, just the extra fingers and toes.

- My family adore you but not your family I'm afraid.

- I could introduce you to my mother, but
  you'd need to take elocution lessons.

- My family say they'll disinherit me if I marry
  you, and I couldn't bear you to be poor.

ARGUMENTS

Traditionally, gentlemen only start arguments that they mean to settle with pistols at dawn.

Gentlemen do not start or become involved in pub brawls.

Gentlemen do not raise their voices in public.

Gentlemen never start arguments with the fairer sex. Should an argument arise, however, gentlemen always concede the final word.

Gentlemen never, ever hit women, and should intercede if they are ever present when a woman is attacked.

A couple drove down a country road for several miles, not saying a word. An earlier discussion had led to an argument and neither of them wanted to concede their position.

As they passed a barnyard of mules, jack asses, and pigs, the husband asked sarcastically, 'Relatives of yours?'

'Yep,' the wife replied, 'in-laws.'

A husband and wife were involved in a petty argument, both of them unwilling to admit they might be in error.

'I'll admit I'm wrong,' the wife told her husband in a conciliatory attempt, 'if you'll admit I'm right.'

He agreed and, like a gentleman, he insisted she go first.

'I'm wrong,' she said.

With a twinkle in his eye, he responded, 'You're right!'

RULES OF THE BEDROOM

A gentleman should know how to seduce
a lady, even when she is obviously willing
to go to bed with him straight away.

Set the scene. Make sure in advance that your
bedroom is tidy and in good order. Yesterday's
socks under the duvet, and cola tins overflowing
with cigarette buts by the bed are not a turn on.
Clean sheets, without holes in them, are a must. If
the bedroom is less than perfect, and you can light
a real fire you may use the hearthrug, although
not the sofa or the sitting-room floor. (Gentlemen
don't have lounges or settees by the way.)

Ladies like firelight, candles and
dimmed lights. It makes them feel more
comfortable about getting naked.

RULE 2

Gentlemen know how to remove
knickers and brassieres with panache.
Finger fumbles are a no-no. If you
aren't much cop at this, study the items
in a lingerie department under the
pretence of buying underwear for your
girlfriend. Don't practise on the manikins,
however, or you might get arrested.

Gauge the lady's feelings. Some women
love a bodice-ripping affair, while
others will be mortified if you tear
the buttons off a new and expensive
item of clothing. Some women might
find you altogether too forward.

Be safe, slow it down.

Remember that a woman consists of more than breasts and a vagina.

She might like her back stroked, her neck kissed, to be spoken to (this may be different from talked dirty to) etc.

Be imaginative.

Learn how to locate the clitoris.

Ask her if you are pleasuring her. She'll usually help you along quite happily.

RULE 6

If you must mention names, make sure it's hers.

RULE 7

Don't suggest kinky sex, bondage rituals, threesomes etc. unless you are 100% sure she's up for it.

RULE 8

Gentlemen never spill the beans on former lovers. This is not the time to ask her about hers either.

RULE 9

Gentlemen think of England.
Make sure she comes first.

RULE 10

Gentleman remember her name in the morning.

Should you forget her name, ask her if she has a nickname or pet name, or whether her mother or father chose her name. She might well mention her true name in her answer.

If that fails, try using terms of endearment such as sexpot, honey bun, or darling. It might seem a little too intimate; on the other hand it might save your bacon – from being hurled at you.

Above all, don't guess.

Did you know…?

The average duration of sexual intercourse for humans is two minutes.

The Italian says, 'When I've a finisheda makina da love with my girlfriend I go down and gently tickle the back of her knees, she floatsa 6 inches abovea da bed in ecstasy.'

The Frenchman replies, 'Zat is nothing, when Ah 'ave finished making ze love with ze girlfriend, Ah kiss all ze way down her body and zen Ah lick zer soles of her feet wiz mah tongue and she floats 12 inches above ze bed in pure ecstasy.'

The Aussie says, 'Mate, that's nothing. When I've finished shaggin my chick, I get out of bed, walk over to the window and wipe my dick on the curtains. And MATE . . she hits the f****** roof.'

10 THINGS A GENTLEMAN SHOULD NEVER SAY WHILE IN BED WITH A LADY

1. On second thoughts, let's turn off the lights.

2. Hope you're as good looking when I'm sober . . .

3. You're almost as good as my ex!

4. You look younger than you feel.

5. And to think, I didn't even have to buy you dinner!

6. What are you planning to make for breakfast?

7. I was so horny tonight I would have taken a duck home!

8. I really hate women who think sex actually means something!

9. You can cook, too, right?

10. How long do you plan to be 'almost there'?

USEFUL MAXIMS

'Talk to every woman as if you loved her, and to every man as if he bored you, and at the end of your first season you will have the reputation of possessing the most perfect social tact.'
Oscar Wilde

'Men who don't understand women fall into two groups: Bachelors and Husbands.'
Jacques Languirand

*'Every woman is wrong until she cries,
and then she is right, instantly.'*
Anon

*'All women become like their mothers.
That is their tragedy. No man does.
That's his.'*
Oscar Wilde

DAY 5
EDUCATION FOR GENTLEMEN

*'A gentleman always remembers
a woman's birthday but never
remembers her age.'*
Anon

Gentleman, sadly, can be stupid but should
try their best not to be so. Education and
refinement should be acquired by all gentlemen
– preferably in a boarding school. This is where
little boys are shipped off to learn that…

- **It is not the done thing to miss mummy.**

- **Bullying by bigger boys begets
  strength of character.**

- **Shorts don't keep one's legs warm in winter.**

- **Soggy biscuit games teach you to
  win or lose with good grace.**

If you haven't been to such an institution, don't
pretend you have. As Jeffery Archer found out,
fiction can be separated from fact without too much
difficulty. On the other hand you are probably safe
in claiming to have been to a good grammar school.

EXERCISE 1: QUOTATIONS

As Sir Winston Churchill said, it is a good
thing for an uneducated man to read books
of quotations. Learn a few and let them slip
occasionally into conversation. If you don't get
them quite right, that's actually OK. It is not
gentlemanly to cite the words of others verbatim.
To do so is to demonstrate a lack of interpretation,
and may be mistaken for vulgar superiority.

Useful quotations

**That which is not good for the beehive cannot
be good for the bees. - Marcus Aurelius**

**Necessity, who is the mother
of invention... - Plato**

**Wind buffs up empty bladders;
opinion, fools. - Socrates**

**Neither cast ye your pearls before swine.
- St. Matthew, New Testament**

**If you are at Rome live in the Roman
style; if you are elsewhere live as they
live elsewhere. - St. Ambrose**

EXERCISE 2: COURSEWORK

TOPIC 1 - HOW TO FILL UP THE ICE CUBE TRAYS. STEP BY STEP, WITH SLIDE PRESENTATION.

TOPIC 2 - THE TOILET PAPER ROLL: DO THEY GROW ON THE HOLDERS? ROUND TABLE DISCUSSION.

TOPIC 3 - IS IT POSSIBLE TO URINATE USING THE TECHNIQUE OF LIFTING THE SEAT UP AND AVOIDING THE FLOOR/WALLS AND NEARBY BATHTUB? GROUP DISCUSSION.

TOPIC 4 – THE FUNDAMENTAL DIFFERENCES BETWEEN THE LAUNDRY HAMPER AND THE FLOOR. PICTURES AND EXPLANATORY GRAPHICS.

TOPIC 5 - THE AFTER-DINNER DISHES AND SILVERWARE: CAN THEY LEVITATE AND FLY INTO THE KITCHEN SINK? EXAMPLES ON VIDEO.

TOPIC 6 - LOSS OF IDENTITY: LOSING THE REMOTE TO YOUR SIGNIFICANT OTHER. HELPLINE SUPPORT AND SUPPORT GROUPS.

TOPIC 7 - LEARNING HOW TO FIND THINGS, STARTING WITH LOOKING IN THE RIGHT PLACE INSTEAD OF TURNING THE HOUSE UPSIDE DOWN WHILE SCREAMING. OPEN FORUM.

TOPIC 8 - HEALTH WATCH: BRINGING HER FLOWERS IS NOT HARMFUL TO YOUR HEALTH. GRAPHICS AND AUDIO TAPE.

TOPIC 9 – DO REAL MEN ASK FOR DIRECTIONS WHEN LOST? REAL LIFE TESTIMONIALS.

TOPIC 10 - IS IT GENETICALLY IMPOSSIBLE TO SIT QUIETLY AS SHE PARALLEL PARKS? DRIVING SIMULATION.

TOPIC 11 - LEARNING TO LOOK AFTER YOURSELF: BASIC DIFFERENCES BETWEEN MOTHER AND WIFE. ONLINE CLASS AND ROLE PLAYING.

TOPIC 12 - HOW TO BE THE IDEAL SHOPPING COMPANION. RELAXATION. EXERCISES, MEDITATION AND BREATHING TECHNIQUES.

TOPIC 13 - HOW TO FIGHT CEREBRAL ATROPHY: REMEMBERING BIRTHDAYS, ANNIVERSARIES, OTHER IMPORTANT DATES AND CALLING WHEN YOU'RE GOING TO BE LATE. CEREBRAL SHOCK THERAPY SESSIONS AND FULL LOBOTOMIES OFFERED.

EXERCISE 3: POETRY WORKSHOP

Gentlemen should know a poem or two from
the first word to the last. Unfortunately the
following examples are neither gentlemanly
nor up to scratch, demonstrating as they
do a weakness in the use of rhyme.

> Mary had a little lamb
> She also had a duck
> She put them on the mantelpiece
> to see if they would
> Fall off.

> Humpty Dumpty sat on a wall
> Humpty Dumpty had a great fall
> All the kings horses and all the kings men
> Said fuck him! – he's only an egg!

> Little boy blew
> Hey! He needed the money!

EXERCISE 4: MATHS FOR MEN

Pick the number of times a week that you would like to have sex (must be more than once but less than 10).

Multiply this number by 2. (That's promising.)

Add 5. (To cover Friday and Saturday night.)

Multiply by 50 (In your dreams!).

We'll just pause here while you find a calculator.

If you have already had your birthday this year add 1755.

If you haven't add 1754.

Now subtract the four-digit year that you were born. (Don't lie or it won't work!)

You should now have a three-digit number.

The first digit of this was your original number. The next two numbers are your age!

EXERCISE 5: WHEN IN ROME

Gentlemen are cultured creatures.
For example they know that:

- When in Japan you wear a kimono left over right.
  (Only corpses wear a kimono right over left.)

- When in Malaysia you eat with your fingers.

- When in Russia refusing to drink is unacceptable.

- When in Thailand feet (which are considered dirty)
  should not be pointed directly at people or raised.

- When in China staring is quite
  common and acceptable.

- When in Albania for 'yes' one shakes the
  head slowly from left to right. To indicate
  'no', one nods briefly up and down.

- When in Algeria pressing a flat right hand to
  the heart shows appreciation or thanks.

- And finally, when in Germany pushing,
  shoving, and other displays of impatience
  in queues are acceptable behaviour.

Gentlemen must eat what they are served
at a foreign banquet with good grace – be
it eyeballs, dog, horse or snake.

Gentlemen should be familiar with
national anthems, songs and dances, and
know what national flags look like.

*'Because of their cuisine, Germans
don't consider farting rude. They'd
certainly be out of luck if they did.'*
P.J. O'Rourke

*'I do not know the American
gentleman, God forgive me for putting
two such words together.'*
Charles Dickens

EXERCISE 6: DRAW THE UNION
JACK IN THE SPACE BELOW

Answer on p. 153

EXERCISE 7: RECITE THE SECOND VERSE OF THE NATIONAL ANTHEM

Answer on p. 154

THINGS YOU SHOULD KNOW ABOUT THE NATIONAL ANTHEM

'God Save the Queen' was originally 'God Save the King'.

The anthem has never been officially adopted by Royal Proclamation or Act of Parliament.

The first public performance of the song is now believed to be when Henry Carey sang it during a dinner in 1740 in honour of Admiral Edward Vernon.

Traditionally, the first performance is thought to have been in 1745, when it was sung in support of George II after the defeat of his army at the Battle of Prestonpans.

Some 140 composers, including Beethoven, Haydn and Brahms, have used the tune in their compositions.

Our National Anthem is not Jerusalem, which is a poem written by William Blake.

EXERCISE 8: USING THE GENTS

When other gentlemen are using the gentlemen's
facilities, it is eyes front at all times. Gentlemen
do not write their friends' telephone numbers
on the lavatory walls, and should have a better
grasp of grammar than to write such things
as 'Pete and Ray woz ere. I weren't.'

*'From now on, ending a sentence with
a preposition is something up with
which I will not put.'*
Sir Winston Churchill

FURTHER REFERENCE: FILMS AND BOOKS

Gentleman Jim

Gentleman's Agreement

The League of Extraordinary Gentlemen

The League of Gentlemen

The Word of a Gentleman

Gentlemen Prefer Blondes

The Sex Diary of a Victorian Gentleman

The Compleat Gentleman

An Officer and a Gentleman

What's Your Calling?

Suitable Employment for Gentlemen etc.

'A successful man is one who makes more money than his wife can spend.'
Anon

Even in the heyday of the English country house, there were not enough of them to go round, and if big brother got to inherit it and the fat of its land, you had to find gainful employment. Gentlemen could join the army, join the navy or join the church for example, or marry an heiress.

Please note that being able to afford not to work is a little different from not wanting to work. On the other hand gentlemen should never gain a reputation for working too hard. And by the way, gentlemen never live within their means.

GENTLEMEN WILL PROBABLY BE PREJUDICED AGAINST THE FOLLOWING CAREERS:

Dustman
Milkman
Builder
Plumber
Road worker
Lorry driver
Taxi driver
Miner
Waiter
Cleaner
Valet
Painter/decorator
Gasman
Shelf stacker
Fast-food counter person
Door-to-door salesmen
Rock singer.

CAREERS MOST GENTLEMEN WOULD LIKE:

Snoozing in the House of Lords
Page-3 editor
Beauty-pageant judge.

A very, very rich but miserly old gentleman
dies, leaving his fortune to his three sons.

However, in his will it is stipulated
that each son must place his third of
the money in the father's coffin.

The funeral comes and goes.

A year later the three sons dine at their club.

The first son, a doctor, says, 'I have to be
honest, I didn't place all of the money
into father's coffin. I kept five million.'

The second son, a farmer, says, 'Well, I
have to admit that I too kept some of
the cash. Ten million to be exact.'

The third son, a lawyer, says, 'I am ashamed at
you two. I wrote a cheque for the FULL amount!'

CALLING CARDS

'To the unrefined and underbred, the
visiting card is but a trifling bit of paper;
but to the cultured disciple of social law, it
conveys a subtle and unmistakable intelligence.
Its texture, style of engraving, and even
the hour of its leaving combine to place the
stranger, whose name it bears, in a pleasant
or a disagreeable attitude...'

Our Deportment, 1881

Once upon a time men carried calling cards. They spent the day stopping off at other people's clubs and houses (people of whom they approved, you understand), although they didn't necessarily visit anybody. They just wanted to remind people to invite them to dinner and to parties, and, of course, that way they didn't have to take tea with gossipy aunts and husband-hunting spinsters. They carried their cards loose in their pockets. Only ladies carried card cases in those days.

Modern-day business cards are not quite the same thing. However, an aspiring gentleman should always carry them on his person. A discreet case is probably acceptable, but avoid a floridly designed card.

> *'The engraving in simple writing is preferred, and without flourishes.'*
>
> Rules of Etiquette & Home Culture, 1882

CLUBS

It's still true to some extent that who you know gets you places, though whether into Old Boys' Clubs and through 'glass ceilings' these days is less certain. You need to network. Get yourself to the right clubs and societies, the right dinners and play the right games.

SOME CLUBS YOU MIGHT CARE TO JOIN

Almack's, Alpine Club, Army and Navy Club, Arthur's, Bucks Club, Cavalry Club, Eccentric Club, Hurlingham Club, Lansdowne Club, Marylebone Cricket Club (MCC), Royal Automobile Club, Royal Thames Yacht Club, St James's Club, Savile Club, Sloane Club, Travellers Club, United Oxford & Cambridge University Club.

YOU CAN'T BE IN OUR CLUB

The most exclusive gentlemen's clubs are in St James's Street: Boodle's, Brooks' and White's. White's is the oldest. It was founded in 1693 – as a chocolate house. Members have to be proposed and seconded. Votes on who can join are done in secret. Committee members place either a white or black ball in a secret wooden contraption. If you are blackballed, you cannot join.

THINGS YOU SHOULD KNOW ABOUT CLUBS

The playwright Sheridan was blackballed three times on the grounds that his father had been on the stage.

At the Pratt club all the waiters are called George.

The Athaneum has a sign below a nude statue stating that 'Ties must be worn at all times'.

DAY 6
MARRYING WELL, PROPOSING, CRYING OFF, KEEPING THE RING ETC.

Scientists have discovered a food
that diminishes a woman's sex
drive by 90% . . .

It's called a wedding cake.

THE PROPOSAL

Gentlemen should ask the bride-to-be's father for his permission to ask the daughter for her hand (in marriage of course).

Gentlemen buy the ring in advance; they may even have access to a family ring that has come back into circulation. She should like it or lump it; but she probably won't.

Gentlemen get down on one knee. She'll probably laugh.

THE ANNOUNCEMENT

If she agrees, a wedding announcement should be placed in The Times so that people can read about it over breakfast and start fishing for invitations.

MATRIMONIAL BLISS

A woman marries a man expecting
he will change, but he doesn't.

*A man marries a woman expecting
that she won't change and she does.*

*

Marriage is a three-ring circus:

engagement ring, wedding ring, suffering.

*

I married Miss Right.

*I just didn't know her first
name was Always.*

*

I never knew what real happiness
was until I got married;

and then it was too late.

*

A woman worries about the future
until she gets a husband.

*A man never worries about the
future until he gets a wife.*

*

Married men live longer
than single men,

*but married men are a lot
more willing to die.*

*

Any married man should
forget his mistakes;

*there is no use in two people
remembering the same thing.*

*

AN UNGENTLEMANLY APPROACH
TO MATRIMONY

1. Twice a week my wife and I go to a nice restaurant, have a little wine, some good food and companionship. She goes on Tuesday, I go on Friday.

2. We sleep in separate beds. Hers is in London and mine is in New York.

3. I take my wife everywhere, but she keeps finding her way back.

4. I asked my wife where she wanted to go for our anniversary. 'Somewhere I haven't been in a long time!' she said. I suggested the kitchen.

5. We always hold hands. If I let go, she shops.

6. She got a mudpack and looked great for two days. Then the mud fell off.

7. She ran after the dustman, yelling, 'Is it too late give you the rubbish?' The driver said, 'No, jump in!'

8. I haven't spoken to my wife for 18 months. I don't like to interrupt her.

9. The last fight was my fault. My wife asked, 'What's on the TV?' . . . I said, 'Dust!'

10. An old friend asked me if my wife and I were going anywhere for our anniversary. I said I couldn't remember where I left her last time we went away, so probably no.

WHAT YOU WILL BE EXPECTED TO PAY FOR IF YOU GO AHEAD WITH THE WEDDING

- £ Engagement ring for bride
- £ Wedding ring for bride
- £ Wedding gift for bride
- £ Best man's gift
- £ Ushers' gifts
- £ Bride's bouquet
- £ Mothers' corsages
- £ Groom's buttonhole
- £ Best man's buttonhole
- £ Ushers' buttonholes
- £ Marriage licence
- £ Vicar's fee
- £ Rehearsal dinner
- £ Wedding car
- £ Honeymoon.

WHAT TO DO IF YOU CAN'T FACE MARRYING HER ON THE BIG DAY

It used to be the case that gentlemen could get into serious trouble for breaking off an engagement. Such an agreement was formerly regarded as a contract between the parties, and breaking it could lead to an action for 'breach of promise'. It was OK for women to have a change of heart, though.

Nowadays, an engagement is not an enforceable contract, but a man who retracts his offer of marriage might still find himself in deep water.

Here are some things you could try...

- Crash your Porsche and get taken by ambulance to hospital.

- Elope to Gretna Green with her younger sister.

- Send her father single malt and a very large cheque.

- Ask the vicar to have sex with you.

- Phone the best man and remind him that if you don't show the tradition is that he takes your place.

- Fake being kidnapped – or pray for aliens to come and get you.

- Tell her she can keep the ring, to have a good bash, and to take her best friend on the honeymoon.

WHAT TO DO WITH THE ENGAGEMENT RING IF YOU BECOME UNENGAGED

It may be the most beautiful, flawless gem ever to have graced her finger, but if you or she calls off the wedding it's traditional that she immediately returns the ring to you, her former fiancé. (Unless she bought it or inherited it in the first place that is.)

A couple are having marital problems.
They go to a counsellor.

The wife explains to him that there are two
things about her husband that bother her:
He's always picking his nose and he never
lets her get on top when they have sex.

The marriage counsellor asks the
husband to explain this.

The husband replies that before his father
passed away, he gave him two pieces of advice:
Always keep your nose clean and never fuck up.

TIPS FOR A HAPPY MARRIAGE

- Buy flowers.
- Take her shopping.
- Offer to cook occasionally.
- Never forget your anniversary.
- Buy her an eternity ring (after one year these days).
- Buy her a maternity ring for each child she bears.
- Learn to change a nappy.
- Don't mention her stretch marks.
- Don't eye up other women in front of your wife.
- As far as most wives are concerned, mistresses are out of fashion.

Giles asks his wife, Jules, what she would like to celebrate their wedding anniversary.

'Would you like a new fur coat?' he asks.

'Not terribly, darling,' says Jules.

'Well how about a new sports car?' says Giles.

'No, not that either,' she responds.

'What about a new pad in the country?' he suggests.

'No thank you, darling,' says Jules.

'Well what would you like for our anniversary?' Giles asks.

'Giles, above all, I'd like a divorce,' she replies.

'Eh, sorry darling,' says Giles. 'You see, I wasn't planning on spending that much.'

*'A gentleman I could never make him,
though I could make him a lord.'*
James I of England

(James VI of Scotland) to his old nurse (who

begged him to make her son a gentleman).

DAY 7

LEISURELY PURSUITS

AND AN ENGLISHMAN'S HOME IS HIS CASTLE

Whether the gentlemen of leisure should idle
away his time or try a little boxing here and a little
horseriding there, has been subject to debate.
Hunting, shooting and fishing are of course the past-
times associated with the upper classes (supposedly,
gentlemen don't call these sports), along with cricket,
tennis, badminton, archery, polo and rugby.

There's no need to jump into red coats or
tweeds (N.B. the only time a gentleman
should wear shorts is on the sports field), but
in your quest to be a gentleman you really
should swat up a bit on the following.

HUNTING

Once upon a time gentlemen couldn't be bothered
to chase after foxes. However, about 250 years
ago, the aristocracy and landed gentry discovered
that the number of deer and hares had declined
and that they'd pretty much run out of wild
boar and wolves . That's when they set their
sights and their hounds on foxes. Nowadays, of
course, the government has banned the 'sport'.

ENGLISH SHOOTING TIMES

Duck	Sep 1 – Feb 1
Pheasant	Oct 1 - Feb 1
Partridge	Sep 1 - Feb 1
Grouse	Aug 12 - Dec 10
Blackgame	Aug 20 - Dec 10
Common Snipe	Aug 12 - Jan 31
Jack Snipe	Sep 1 - Jan 31
Woodcock	Oct 1 - Jan 31

WHAT TO DO WITH A BRACE OF PHEASANT (THAT'S A MALE AND A FEMALE BIRD, THE MALE BEING THE ONE WITH THE MOST COLOURFUL PLUMAGE)

Hang your pheasant for two weeks. After this period, you'll need to pluck them (that's without resorting to a recital of the pheasant plucker's mate song, if you please).

Take the bird by the feet and hold it head down with wings outspread and breast forward. Gently pull a few feathers away from the breast. Don't be tempted to yank out a handful, you'll just rip the skin and make a mess of things. (Most men are familiar with the difference between a yank and pull.) The whole process should take you half an hour; remember to remove the other inedible bits. Be prepared for mess.

There are many ways in which to cook pheasant. You can grill, roast, casserole, sauté, sear or smoke the thing, or how about braising it in gin and juniper? Do watch out for shot when you are eating pheasant, or you will find yourself with a painful tooth.

If you want to cheat, your local butcher may do the job for you for a price. If you are on a shoot, you may find that there is access to a plucking machine, which will do the job in a minute. If you are half way through the job and have cocked it up, rip off the entire skin and cover flesh with slices of bacon.

TAKING THE BAIT: FISHING

If you want to be a gentleman and your knowledge of British fish is cod and chips, you've got your work cut out. Still – spare the rod and you'll spoil the gentleman. Get thee to an angling club.

Some fish you could have caught in British lakes and rivers:
Salmon, trout, carp, tench, bream, roach, rudd, perch, pike, orfe, chub, ide, gudgeon, catfish, eel.

Some fish you won' t have caught in British lakes and rivers:
Kippers (these are smoked herring), caviare (these are the eggs of the sturgeon), shark, tuna, swordfish, clownfish, koi carp (unless you've been fishing in someone's fish pond).

N.B.

Know thy poundage – you are very unlikely to have caught a 30-lb rudd.

Koi are not big goldfish. The goldfish is a but a distant cousin.

HOW TO PLAY CRICKET

Teams are made up of 11 players each.

They play with a small, hard, red ball that leaves red marks down the players' white trousers.

Players dress in cricket whites. The ball is hit with a long wooden bat. Two batters stand in front of wickets, set about 20 metres apart.

Each wicket consists of three wooden sticks (stumps) pushed into the ground, with two small pieces of wood (bails) balanced on top.

A member of the opposing team (the bowler) throws the ball towards one of the batters, who must hit the ball so that it does not knock a bail off the wicket.

If the ball travels far enough, the two batters run back and forth between the wickets while the fielders on the opposing team try to catch the ball.

The game is scored according to the number of runs, which is the number of times the batters exchange places.

Cricket is not cricket without stopping for tea.

SPORTING TALK

*'Rugby is a beastly game
played by gentlemen;
soccer is a gentlemen's game
played by beasts;
football is a beastly game
played by beasts.'*
Henry Blaha

*'The English country
gentleman galloping after
a fox – the unspeakable in full
pursuit of the uneatable.'*
Oscar Wilde

'Serious sport has nothing to do with fair play. It is bound up with hatred, jealousy, boastfulness, disregard of all rules and sadistic pleasure in witnessing violence. In other words, it is war minus the shooting.'
George Orwell

'*When a man wants to murder a tiger,
he calls it sport; when the tiger wants
to murder him, he calls it ferocity.*'
George Bernard Shaw

'*The fascination of shooting as a sport
depends almost wholly on whether
you are at the right or wrong end of
the gun.*'
P. G. Wodehouse

'There's a fine line between
fishing and just standing on
the shore like an idiot.'
Steven Wright

'A good walk spoiled.'
Mark Twain (on golf)

CASTLE TRIVIA

Edward II got impaled at Berkeley
castle – the red-hot-poker up
the backside case – allegedly for
preferring gentlemen to ladies.

The Queen hates
Buckingham Palace.

Charles I was imprisoned at
Carisbrooke Castle on the
Isle of Wight. The castle
chapel is dedicated to St.
Charles The Martyr.

AN ENGLISHMAN'S HOME IS HIS CASTLE

ENGLISH CASTLES

Arundel, Beeston, Berkeley, Carisbrooke, Dover, Eynsford, Framlingham, Goodrich, Hastings, Kenilworth, Lindisfarne, Minster Lovell, Nottingham , Old Sarum, Portchester, Rochester, Sherborne, Tintagel, Windsor, York.

CONCLUSION

Do you call yourself a gentleman now?
Well you shouldn't, because gentlemen
do not refer to themselves as such.

REMEMBER, IT WOULD NOT BE GENTLEMANLY TO SAY TO YOUR PARTNER...

- If I can learn to work the toilet seat, so can you: if it's up, put it down.

- You never buy me flowers either.

- That tux is but a fraction of what you spent on shoes this month.

- If you ask me if you're bum looks big in those jeans, expect me to lie.

- You'll be glad to hear that we're going fishing for the weekend.

- Dogs are better than cats: foxes kill cats; dogs kill foxes.

- I believe in God – Sunday's a day of rest.

- Crying is blackmail.

- Idle chatter is vulgar. 'Yes' and 'No' are perfectly acceptable answers.

- Nothing says 'I love you' more than sex in the morning.

*'Waste no more time arguing about
what a good man should be.
Be one.'*
Marcus Aurelius

THE UNION JACK

Answer to exercise 6, p. 110

light grey shading = red

dark grey shading = blue

VERSE 2 OF 'GOD SAVE THE QUEEN'

Answer to excersise 7, p. 111

Thy choicest gifts in store
On her be pleased to pour,
Long may she reign.
May she defend our laws,
And give us ever cause,
To sing with heart and voice,
God save the Queen.

CREDITS

www.trumpers.com

North West League Against Cruel
Sports Support Group

Wikepedia, www.wikipedia.org

www.britcastles.com/englcas.htm

How To Tie A Bow Tie from Bridal Guide Magazine

Other Crombie Jardine books that may be of interest

The Little Book of ASBOs
Asbolent Behaviour from around the UK
1-905102-41-0, £2.99

The Bumper Book of Lies
1-905102-37-2, £8.99

The Little Book of Chavs
The Branded Guide to Britain's New Elite
1-905102-01-1, £2.99

Everything I Know About Men
I Learnt From My Dog
1-905102-25-9, £9.99

Getting Old is When...

A Light-Hearted Look at the Aging Process

1-905102-39-9, £4.99

The Little Book of Pervs

True Sexual Weirdness from the World's News

1-905102-38-0, £2.99

Shag Your Way to the Top

The Real Fast Track to Success

1-905102-17-8, £2.99

The Little Book of Stupid Drunks

A Year's Worth of real-Life Drunken
Mayhem from the World's News

1-905102-23-2, £2.99

All Crombie Jardine books are available from your
High Street bookshops, Amazon, Littlehampton Book
Services, or Bookpost (P.O.Box 29, Douglas,
Isle of Man, IM99 1BQ.
tel: 01624 677 237, email: bookshop@enterprise.
net. Free postage and packing within the UK).

Please send your comments suggestions
to: jeeves@crombiejardine.com

www.crombiejardine.com